# Fun Activities For Clever Kids

The book belongs To

_______________________

WELCOME
HOME

1
2
3
Dog

PET SHOP

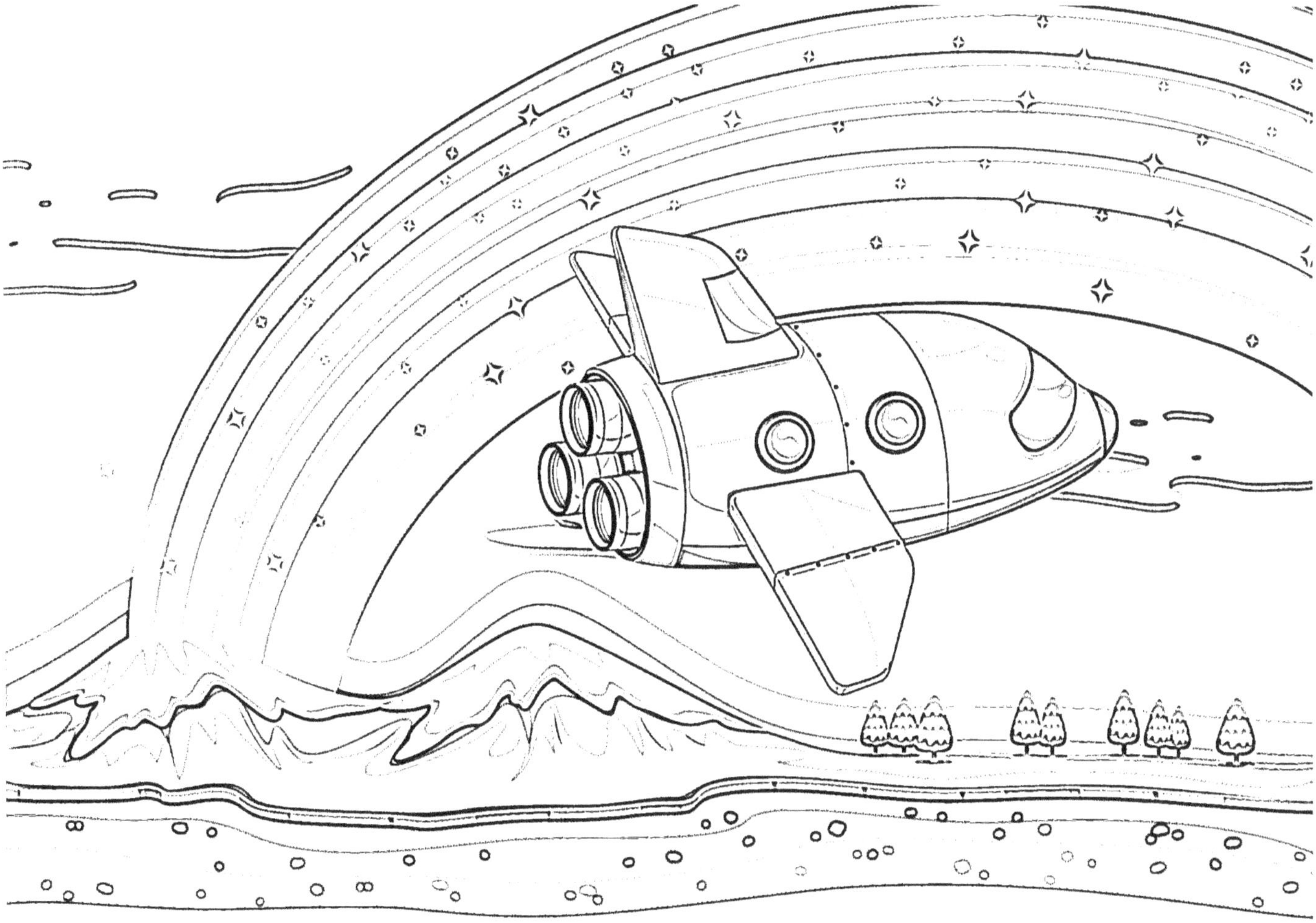

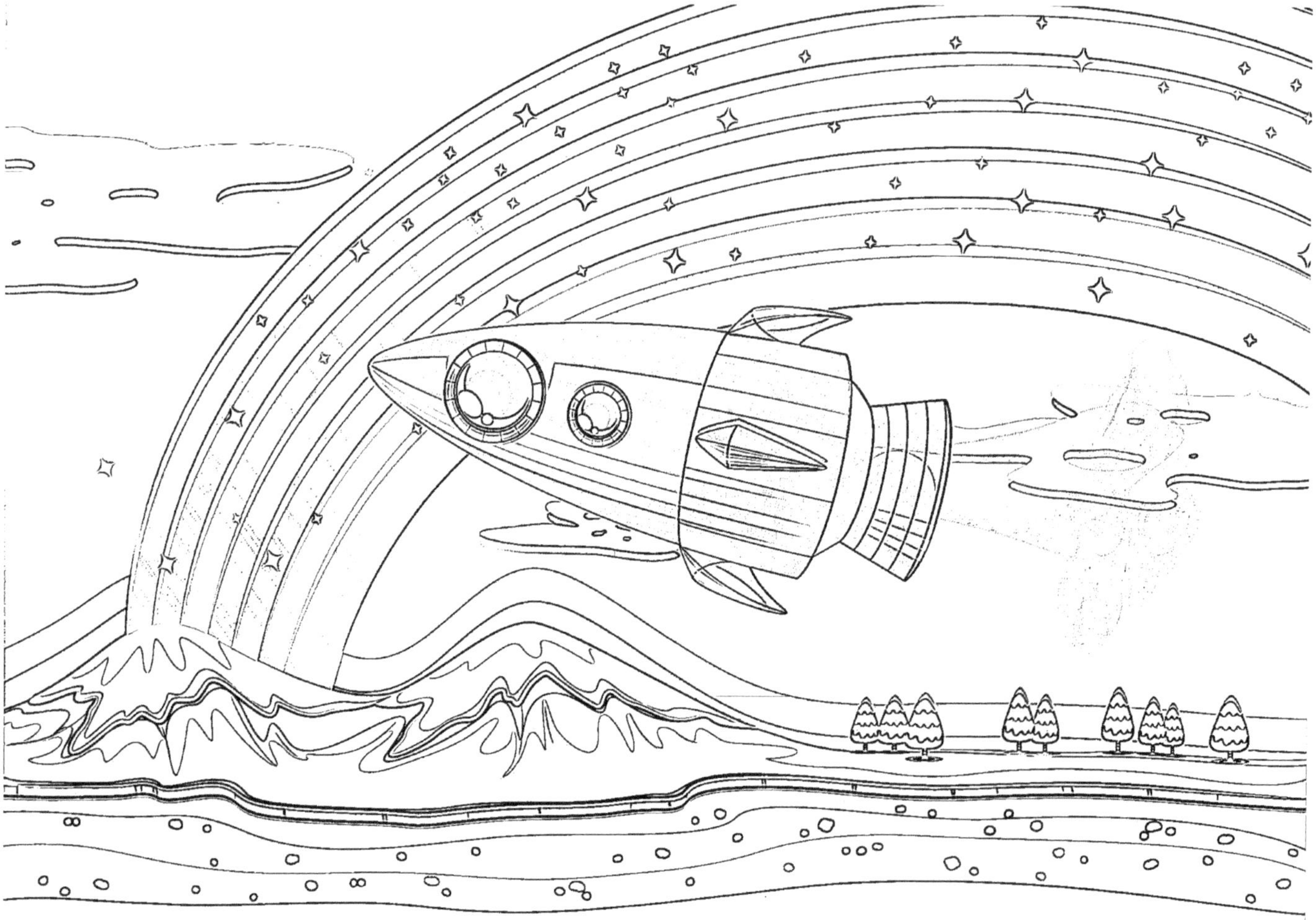

# Help the pirate find his treasure!

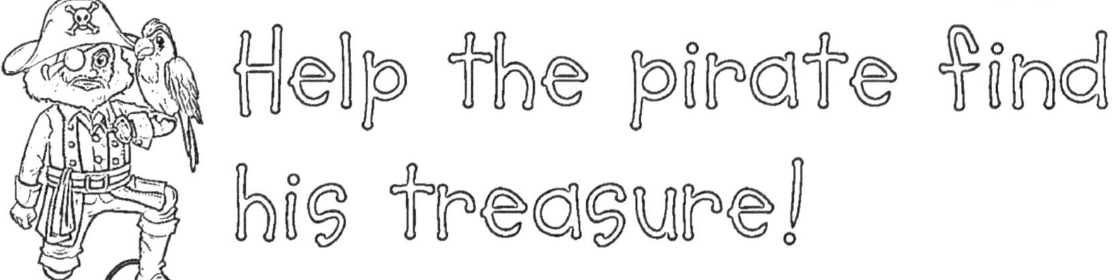

Honey

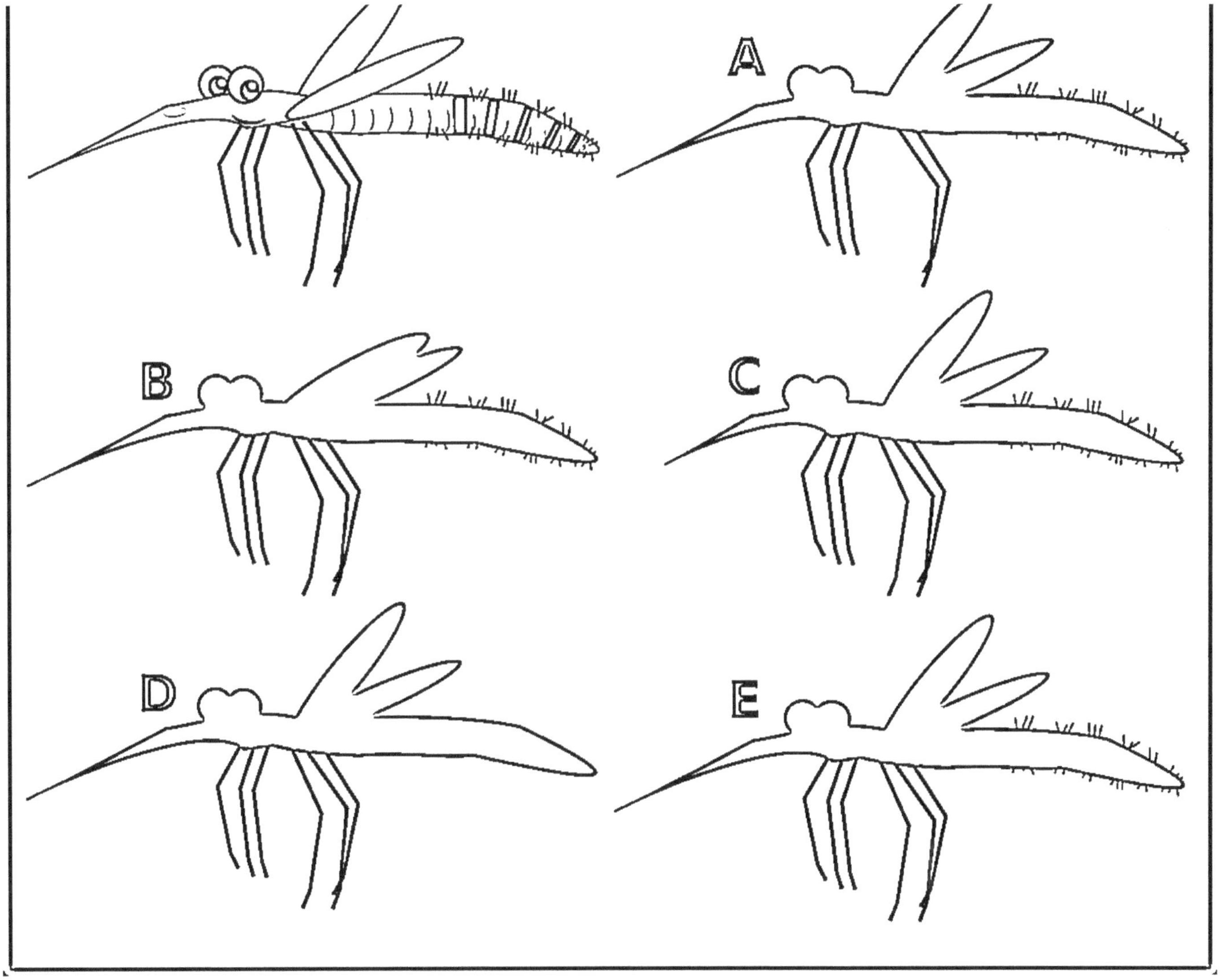

PET
SHOP

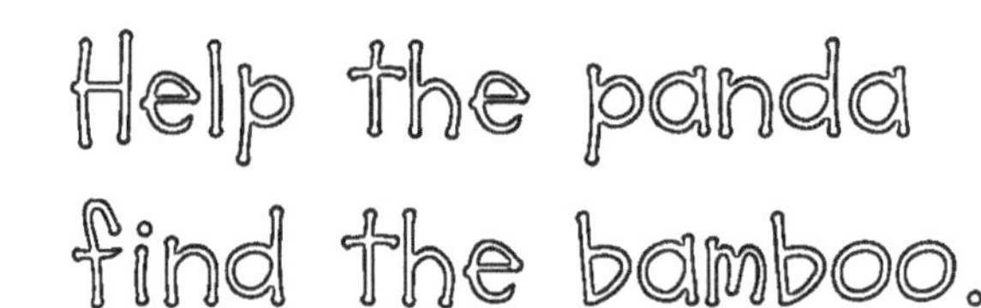

Help the panda
find the bamboo.

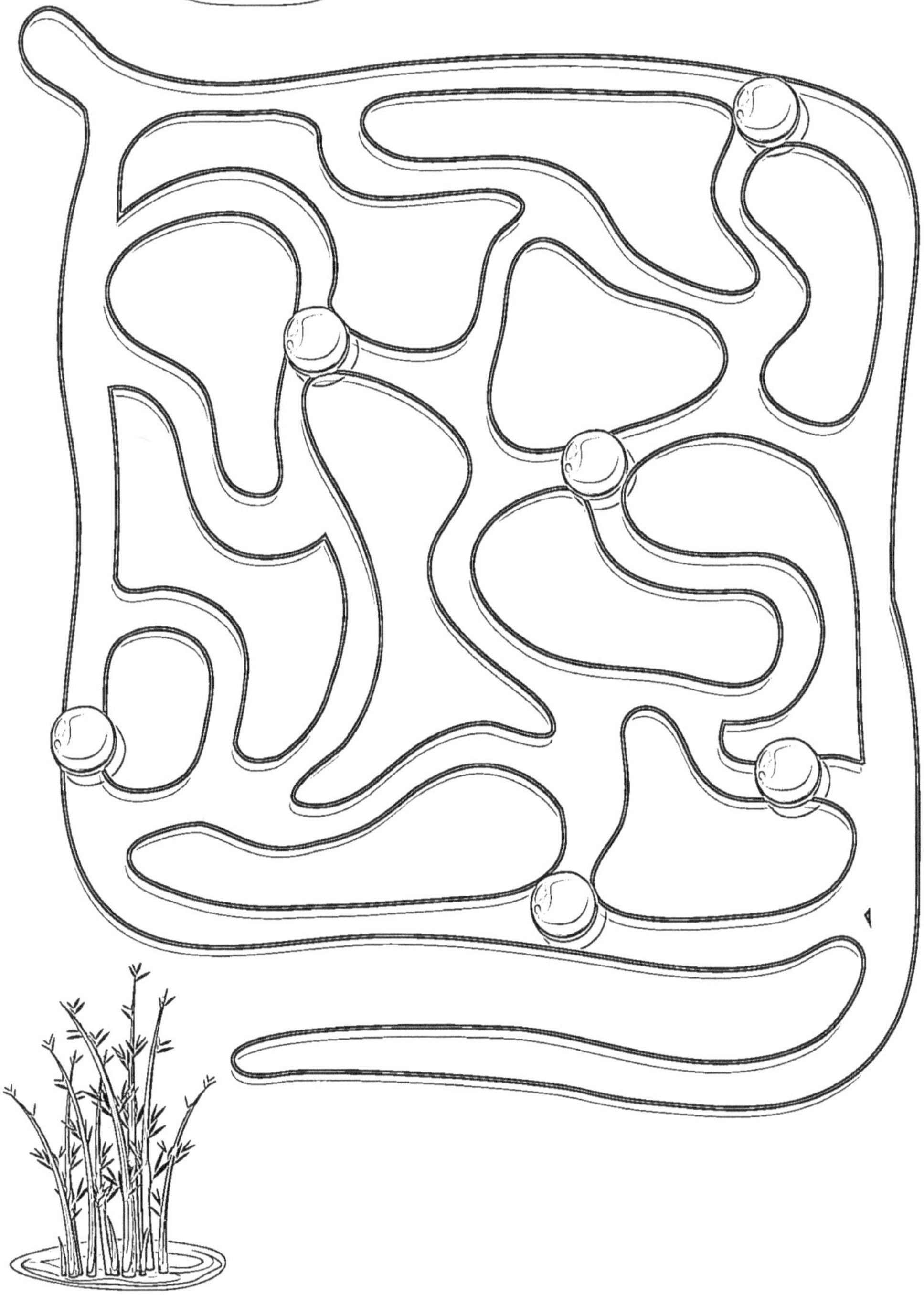

Help the king
find his castle.